TEN
GUIDELINES
FOR MAKING OUR LEANER TEAM
A MEANER ONE

BUILDING STRONG LEADERS
IN THE FACE OF ADVERSITY

Mark L. Barry
Illustrated by John Gilpin

GUIDING STAR
BOOKS

Send feedback to: feedback@lodestarandcompany.com

Published by Guiding Star Books, New London, CT USA

ISBN-13: 978-0692860182
ISBN-10: 0692860185

Mark L. Barry can be reached at the following address:
mbarry@lodestarandcompany.com

John Gilpin can be reached at the following address:
johngilpin@verizon.net

Available from Amazon.com and other retail outlets.
Available on Kindle and other online stores.
www.lodestarandcompany.com
www.TenGuidelines.com

*This book is dedicated
to those individuals
who unknowingly contributed
to its contents.*

Contents

INTRODUCTION

Ten Guidelines for Making Our Leaner Team a Meaner One started out as a few cursory notes for an upcoming meeting. It soon evolved into a protocol that I needed my managers to adopt, as our company would soon enter a period of significant expense reduction.

When one is confronted with a trying and demanding situation such as this, it is natural to feel a sense of urgency to improve worker productivity and morale both measurably and quickly. This feeling of immediacy can sometimes cause a sixth sense to kick in and, with heightened awareness, lead oneself to better identify behaviors that could have a negative and potentially parasitic effect on the company's ability to succeed.

Ten Guidelines represents a compilation of the more troubling behaviors that I have witnessed over time. The statements were heard in conference rooms, over business lunches and dinners, during quarterly meetings, and in hallways. Curiously, they emitted from the mouths of both inexperienced and skilled employees, seasoned executives, and members of top management.

The disconcerting statements presented in this book are direct quotes, and each are followed by a recommended alternative approach that is far more positive and productive in nature. Given that we learn business behaviors by noticing the examples set by others around us, *Ten Guidelines* offers an encouraging and shared "Let's all act this way" approach. I have found that this inclusive style helps the guidelines gain traction soon after being put into practice.

In fact, when we got to the other side of our expense reductions and reflected on our journey and results, it was evident that my staff had embraced the guidelines and accomplished much more than the operational task at hand.

Each of them had succeeded in growing – as individuals and as leaders – and the company was much stronger as a result. It is worth noting that *Ten Guidelines* works equally well in periods of expansion, which is why I continue to stress them with the companies and executives whom I am fortunate to advise.

If you are a business person looking for a quick read of clever and pithy phrases, this is not the guidebook for you. If you are concerned, however, about getting more positive and productive energies out of yourself and those around you, then you have found your tool.

Just remember that whether you are a CEO or a front-line employee, everyone can fall prey to the traps mentioned herein. So, read the guidelines twice…memorize them once…and utilize them always. You might even find that the guidelines work well outside of the office, too.

M.L.B.

TEN

GUIDELINES

FOR MAKING OUR LEANER TEAM
A MEANER ONE

BUILDING STRONG LEADERS
IN THE FACE OF ADVERSITY

-1-

BE
OPEN

If we say,

"I tried that before
and it didn't work" . . .

we might be shortchanging

a good idea.

The "Be Open" Approach

Let's take the position that a
different set of people, working
under a different set of circumstances
and with a different plan,
may yield different results.

-2-

BE
RESPONSIBLE
& FOLLOW
THROUGH

If we say,

"I didn't know whom to ask" . . .

there is a good chance we are either

taking too long to solve problems

or not solving many at all.

The "Be Responsible & Follow Through" Approach

Let's agree that time is too short and too valuable to waste. Merely thinking about correcting a situation – and not acting on it – will not make the problem go away and may make it worse.

-3-

BE
A TEAM
PLAYER

If we say,

"That's not part of my job" . . .

we are not displaying shared ownership

in the success of this company.

The "Be a Team Player" Approach

If we see a coworker in need of assistance, let's provide a hand. If we see a crumpled piece of paper on the hallway floor, let's pick it up.

-4-

BE CANDID

If we say,

"I didn't want to ask her because

she'd be shocked that I didn't

know the answer" . . . we are not

acting our ages.

The "Be Candid" Approach

Let's drop our pants. We will never get
to a higher level of productivity if we
choose to bypass learning something new
for fear we might expose a shortcoming
in the process.

-5-

BE
PROACTIVE
& PERSISTENT

If we say,

"I put a plan together six months

ago, but then I started working

on other projects" . . .

we need to work harder at

implementing our ideas.

The "Be Proactive & Persistent" Approach

Not implementing a sound plan
after spending time creating it is like
eating chocolate cake immediately
after running five miles. Let's not waste
our efforts. In recognizing that initiatives
do not always take flight as quickly
as we would like, let's return our plans
to the foreground regularly.

-6-

BE
PROFESSIONAL

If we say,

"I'm going over to his office

to give him a piece of my mind" . . .

we have forgotten where we work.

The "Be Professional" Approach

Let's conduct our daily interactions
with coworkers with the same
level of professionalism
that we display when dealing with
customers or representatives
from outside businesses.

-7-

BE
A MOTIVATOR

If we say,

"My objectives are on track,

and that's all I care about" . . .

we may find that down the road

we are men and women

without a country.

The "Be a Motivator" Approach

Let's take charge of our own backyard and work to motivate our neighbors to follow suit. That way, we all win.

-8-

BE
DIRECT

If we say,

"I sent you a really long email,

so you'd be fully informed" . . .

we mistakenly think recipients will

read past the opening sentence.

The "Be Direct" Approach

Let's boil our thoughts down to a
single theme. Writing with clarity
and brevity better ensures
that our messages will be both
read and understood.

-9-

BE
A LISTENER

If we say,

"Sure. Yep. Uh huh. No Problem" . . .

we may be doing a lot more

hearing than listening.

The "Be a Listener" Approach

Let's recognize that, at any given moment,
we all have a dozen things on our mind.
If someone takes the time to share an idea
or express a need, listen to comprehend.
Effective communication requires
at least two active parties.

-10-

BE
A LEADER

If we say,

"These 10 guidelines don't work

for me" . . . we will have a decent chance

of neither getting along well with others

nor achieving our business objectives.

The "Be a Leader" Approach

Let's work within these guidelines because leadership is not synonymous with a title printed on a business card. Fostered only by our actions, it is a perception that is developed over time by those around us.

Mark L. Barry is a strategic business advisor, who is committed to enabling organizations and business owners to identify and seize growth opportunities in the marketplace.

John Gilpin is a cartoonist and Legion of Honor recipient, whose illustrations have appeared on the covers and pages of more than 400 magazines and newspapers worldwide.

NOTES

NOTES

Notes

NOTES

NOTES

NOTES

NOTES

Made in the USA
Columbia, SC
18 May 2017